Other works by Jim Heynen

Maedra Poems, 1974, Peaceweed Press
Notes from Custer, 1976, Bear Claw Press
Sioux Songs (translations), 1976, Blue Cloud Press
The Funeral Parlor, 1976, Graywolf Press
How the Sow Became a Goddess, 1977, Confluence Press

JIM HEYNEN

THE MAN WHO KEPT
CIGARS IN HIS CAP

WITH ILLUSTRATIONS BY

TOM POHRT

GRAYWOLF PRESS

Grateful acknowledgement is due to the editors of the following magazines where most of these tales first appeared, some in slightly different form: *Kayak, Poetry Now, Zero, Field, Portland Review, Kuksu, Sunday Clothes,* and *Carleton Miscellany.*

Special thanks to the National Endowment for the Arts, the U.S. State Department, and the British Council for their assistance through the U.S.-U.K. Bicentennial Exchange Fellowship to England where this book was completed.

LC number 77-95332
ISN 0-915308-17-7 (paper)
      0-915308-18-5 (cloth)

Graywolf Press, PO Box 142, Port Townsend, WA 98368

CONTENTS

III   Bloating and Its Remedies

THE MAN WHO KEPT
CIGARS IN HIS CAP

I

The Man Who Kept
Cigars in His Cap

WHO BUILT A LOT OF SHEDS

Down the road was a man who was an odd one. He built 70 sheds on his farm. Little sheds where he could put little things everyone figured could go somewhere else. Whenever he had something he wanted to put away, instead of looking for a place for it in one of his buildings, he built a special little shed to put it in. When he bought a new lawn mower, he built a new shed for it. When his dog had 8 puppies, he built 8 little dog houses for the new animals. He had a little shed where he put tin cans. He had one for old shoes. He had one for chicken feathers.

And one shed, away back in the grove, painted bright red with white trim, was his secret shed.

What does he keep in that red shed in the grove, everyone wondered.

The boys sneaked out there to find out, but the red shed had a big lock on it. And no windows to see through.

So they went to the man and asked him, What do you have in your red shed in the grove? He was a friendly man, so they thought it would be all right to ask.

But the man got angry when the boys asked him this and he said, That is none of your business, none at all.

When the boys went back to check the shed again, the man had put another lock on the door and a sign that said KEEP OUT.

Let's climb up in the trees and wait. Maybe he'll come by and unlock the door, said one of the boys.

They climbed the trees and sat on branches where they could see the man's red shed.

Pretty soon he came out there and unlocked the door. And opened it.

Inside was another shed! A blue one, that had a lock on its door too. Then he opened the door of the blue shed and inside was a smaller yellow shed! And inside that a green one! The man was down on his knees opening door after door of his little sheds. Pretty soon the boys couldn't see where his hand was going. And all those little sheds, one after another, looked like a rainbow, and the boys couldn't see where it ended.

THE MAN WHO KEPT CIGARS
IN HIS CAP

One man kept cigars in his cap. When the boys sneaked up behind him during threshing and tipped it off, the cigars fell on the ground. This was very funny to everyone, until one day the man put a rat in his cap. It was a rat the man had fed eggs so it was friendly to him.

When the boys tipped off his cap this time, the rat jumped to the ground and frightened them so that they screamed and looked foolish.

The boys said, He can't do this to us! We're boys from Welcome #3! Which was their township and schoolhouse number.

So they found a big tom cat that liked to kill rats. They took a striped engineer's cap like the cigar man wore and put a rubber rat under it and taught the tom cat to find the rat.

After a while they went walking toward the threshing machine where the man was working. One of the boys carried the tom cat on his shoulder, and no one paid attention when they walked behind the man. The tom cat saw the engineer's cap and jumped at it as the boys had taught him to do.

But instead of a rat, the man had put a skunk under the cap. It was an orphan skunk the man had fed milk when it was a baby, so the skunk was friendly to the man.

When the tom cat landed on the man's hat, the skunk let go its spray in the cat's eyes and on the heads of the boys. Everybody laughed at the boys as they ran away to the stock tank screaming and crying.

When the boys had cleaned themselves, the biggest one said, He has made us look like fools again. Let's do something to keep him from making everyone laugh at us.

So they started practicing with their sling shots and practiced until they could hit a tin can from 30 yards. They crawled behind a fence where no one could see them.

The man had put an owl under his hat, thinking that this time the boys would have a weasel. It was an owl he had helped in winter when its eyes were frozen shut so the owl was friendly to him.

When the man was not expecting it, the boys shot their stones at his cap. The stones hit the cap, some going through the cloth and through the feathers of the owl, killing it.

No one scolded the boys for killing the owl. Everyone agreed that the man had been asking for trouble right from the start when he put cigars in his cap.

WHO MADE SUCH GOOD PIES

It was always good to visit that lady because she made such good pies. What was so good about them was the little waves on the edge of the crusts. The boys could tell how big a piece they were getting by counting those little waves. A piece of her pie looked like this.

perfect little waves

Eight waves was a big piece.

How does she do it? the other ladies asked. No one knew.

The boys walked over to her house early one day before everyone was going over there for pie. They stood outside her kitchen window and watched her making her pies. This is what they saw.

When the lady had the pie crust rolled out in the pie pan, she reached into her mouth and pulled out her false teeth. Then she took them and pushed them down on the pie crust all the way around. The spaces between her false teeth made all those nice little waves that everybody liked so much.

Pretty soon everyone came for fresh pie.

What beautiful pies! all the ladies said.

The boys got eight-wave pieces that day.

Every now and then, between bites of that good pie, the boys looked at the lady. She was watching everyone eat and grinning a big grin.

THE MAN
WHO SHARPENED SAWS

His old green truck had a soft bump to it when it came down the drive, but the man who sharpened saws was cruel. He'd kick cats or feed steel shavings to the chickens, if they bothered him. Usually they didn't—the boys cleared his way of chickens and hid the cats.

More than cruel, he was a communist. The boys heard that was how he really made his money so they made him a song:

Bumpity bumpity
Here comes the commie
In his old green chevy.

Nobody asked him to come, but when he did, everybody brought their saws and watched him file in his easy way. That sound was music to the boys. At least, the nearest they had ever heard to a violin.

When he finished his filing, he charged a dollar. Once he forgot even that.

That's how everybody knew he was a communist. And there were his tracts the boys might never accept, ones with big pictures of men with picks and shovels.

He's rotten to the core, said one of the men.

But the boys noticed how pure the saws glistened and they'd celebrate his leaving by sawing wood. Any wood. It all was butter to them then.

By spring, when he was almost off their minds, the saws got dull, and the boys could hardly cut a willow branch to make a whistle. So they sang

Bumpity bumpity
NOW where's that commie
In his old green chevy!

It was hard going with a dull saw, but one spring even the men talked about putting up signs to keep him away. And they would have, if they could have found saws sharp enough to make the signs.

THE JEWELER

The jeweler had great big hands. They were maybe twice the size of an average man's and three times the size of a boy's.

What the jeweler liked to do most were the hardest jobs— like replacing the smallest part in a lady's watch or fitting tiny pictures into little girls' lockets. People came to his small store and watched him for hours as he tried to fix little things. He bit his lip and concentrated very hard, but he'd usually squeeze the tiny hinges of a girl's locket so hard that only he would be able to open it when he finished, or he'd break one part of a lady's watch while trying to fix another part and when the lady got her watch back it would either run too fast or too slow or not at all. But the jeweler kept trying and he might have done all right in time if his eyesight had been better.

Somehow, the jeweler prospered in his business. Everyone knew he worked hard and was doing the best he could. No one ever thought of complaining about his work.

Then one day the jeweler's shop was closed. "GONE OUT OF BUSINESS" the sign on the door said in very bad writing, and inside all the shelves were empty.

What happened to our jeweler? everyone wondered. Then word came that the jeweler had moved to a large town in the next county.

This made the people curious, so a few ladies went to see what he was doing and why he had left, though as they drove off several people told them not to ask the jeweler to come back.

The ladies found him in the next county. He had a new shop with a sign that read "HAND-MADE MINIATURE CHRIST-MAS TREE DECORATIONS."

This is what he told the ladies. "Things were good in the jewelry business, you understand. But pretty soon it just wasn't a challenge anymore. I've got to have that challenge, you know."

The jeweler was biting his lip the way the ladies had seen him do when he was working on a very small locket. Now he was trying to glue tiny angel wings the size of a bee's on a tiny wooden body. The wings were crinkling and falling to pieces in his big fingers. Some of his finished decorations were already on display in the shop window—lop-sided little stars and reindeer with legs that were too long or too short and antlers that looked like spaghetti. Worst of all was a little Santa Claus whose tummy, instead of bulging, was indented where the man's big thumb had held him.

Outside, people from the new town were gathering near the ex-jeweler's shop window, looks of pity in their eyes and their hands already reaching into their purses.

The ladies who had come from the old town left without saying anything. They felt it was time to go, even if their watches couldn't tell them so.

THE BOYS GO TO ASK
A NEIGHBOR FOR SOME APPLES

When the boys went to one neighbor's farm to ask him if they might pick some of his apples, they could not find him anywhere. They went to the house, and then to all the buildings and called for him. They checked the machine shed to see if the tractor was out. It wasn't.

They started looking behind things—behind the pig troughs and cattle feeders, behind the fences and wagons. Finally, when they crawled over some hay bales in the barn—in a very dark corner of the barn—they saw him. He was praying to his animals.

On his knees with his hands crossed on his lap. Praying to a piglet, a dog, a cat, and a bull calf. He had fed each of them their own kind of food, so they were quiet as he prayed.

He was saying, Little animals with four feet on the ground, teach the rocks to lie in their places, tell the oceans never to rise and the mountains never to fall. Little ones, give your gentle ways to me.

The boys slipped away and went to wait in the yard. When the man came out of the barn, they asked him about apples. He brought a large basket and said they could fill it with the ripest and largest apples from his trees. Not only that. He said they could keep the basket to carry feed to their animals.

THE GOOSE LADY

Down the road lived an old lady who kept geese in her house. She lived upstairs and the geese lived downstairs. It was funny driving by in a car and honking because this made the old woman and geese look out their windows at the same time. All those long goose necks popped up in the downstairs window and the old lady's head popped up in the upstairs window. The old lady's neck was long too, and she wore a hat—even in the house—that made her head look like a big goose head.

During the day the lady went out into her orchard and picked weeds. She also picked up leaves and little sticks that fell from the trees. Lots of times the geese followed her around in the orchard, looking in all the spots where she picked things up to see if maybe she was really finding food.

The boys were supposed to stay away from the goose lady's house because she was crazy. The boys weren't so sure about that, so they went over there anyhow and watched the goose lady from the ditch.

Something you couldn't hear driving by in a car was that the goose lady was singing.

> Lowly geese, by my side,
> How my sorrow I do hide,
> In the shivering of the leaves,
> In the whining of the bees.
>
> Lonely geese, tell me why
> You never reach toward the sky,
> Where the wind can set you free
> From earth, and free from me.
>
> Lovely geese, do you know
> That the one I once loved so
> Much more than my old eyes tell
> Turned his face and bade farewell?

Lowly geese, by my side,
How my sorrow I do hide,
He left me nothing but an egg
And prayed that I would never beg.

Lovely geese, you've served me well
With eggs to eat and down to sell,
Ever close at my side,
How my sorrow you do hide.

Yep, she's crazy, whispered one of the boys. So they slipped away without the goose lady seeing them.

And they didn't go back. They didn't have to. They had learned her song after hearing it just once. And they sang it to themselves whenever they were doing things they didn't like to do.

WHO STOLE THINGS

One man walked around at night and when people were not at home, he went into their houses and took things. Little things. Cookies. A doily from a coffee table. A bathroom towel. An egg or two. Maybe a pair of old pliers. He might have done this for years without anyone noticing, except that he never used anything he took. So things started cluttering up his house and tool shed, and people saw them when they visited. What's more, his wife was a worrier and asked people if they needed their things back.

In other ways the man was like everyone else. He even taught Sunday School. He also was a good farmer and knew more than most about curing sick chickens.

The boys knew he stole things. They didn't think it was fair that he could steal things, and they didn't like him for it. So one night they went over to his house, and when the lights were out, they sneaked into his tool shed and took a handful of shingle nails. But when they were sneaking out, the man caught them. He must have known what kind of noises a thief makes, so he was waiting for them by the tool shed door.

First he made them put the shingle nails back—he knew just where the boys had found them. Then he gave them all a spanking. With a paddle he had stolen two years before!

Now be good boys and go home, he said.

The boys ran home crying and saying, It's not fair!

When they told their story at home, they got another spanking, even harder than the man had given them, and were sent to bed without another word about it.

THE BREEDING CIRCUIT

Every springtime for many years this man took his stallion Bayard on a breeding circuit. They'd stop at the same farms yearly, the man leading his stallion from one place to the next where the mares would be waiting.

Bayard was a magnificent beast, muscular and spirited and noble in his carriage, yet gentle with the mares. He was the most famous horse in the county, and farmers on his circuit were as proud of the mares Bayard bred as Bayard's master was of his fine stallion. It was said that in time every young horse in the area would look a little bit like Bayard.

And it must have been happy work leading that stallion on the breeding circuit because Bayard's master was always smiling when they left one farm for the next.

When tractors came, farmers started selling their horses for dog and mink feed. A few kept their mares a few years just to have them bred by Bayard, but pretty soon the breeding circuit was a lonely walk. Farmers working the fields with their tractors would see the man and his stallion slowly moving along the road, often stopping to stare at the empty pastures. It was very sad.

Then one year only Bayard's master was walking along the road. One farmer whose mare had been a regular customer in the old days was in the back of his field when he saw the man approaching his farmyard. The farmer felt sorry for him and wondered what had happened to Bayard but did not have the time to leave his field work. Later, when the farmer drove his tractor home for dinner, Bayard's master was just leaving down the driveway to his farm. He was heading toward the next farm on the circuit, still smiling the way he had in the old days.

THE GREAT STRENGTH

There were many strong men. Ones who showed up at county fairs and wrestled a steer. Or went into the ring with the circus wrestler and threw him out in ten seconds. There were men who came to the sales barn every Saturday and took bets on what they could lift. Usually a young steer in one of the pens. Men who took on any two men in tug-of-war. Everyone knew who the strong men were and who to bet on.

But then there was the man nobody noticed. Who never tried showing off in front of people. He was the one with the great strength.

How could you tell who had the great strength? You couldn't. Not until there was an accident. Then he'd be there like the one good spring that never goes dry in a dry year. Just when you needed him he'd be there and not even smiling. Just doing what had to be done, pulling a hand free from moving gears, lifting a wagon off somebody's leg, pulling a hog from a well. Whatever had to be done.

The boys saw the great strength once. Late August when everything was quiet. All the oats harvested. All the straw stacked. Farmers in town visiting.

An old church was being torn down and people were standing around watching. The caterpillar was pushing big pieces out of its side. All of a sudden the wind caught a piece of loose roof and lifted it off the church. It went wobbling through the air like a sick bird, then landed on one end and tipped over on a bunch of people.

When all you could hear was everyone's screaming, the roof started rising slowly, as if the wind had caught it again. It wasn't the wind. It was the great strength, in old overalls, lifting that big section of roof. All of those trapped people were crawling out scratched and bleeding.

Afterwards, everybody was looking out for the people who got hurt under the roof, and after a little while no one knew for sure where the great strength had gone. He was like the wind in this way too.

THE MINISTER'S WIFE

There were two reasons everyone noticed the minister's wife when she walked into church with her children—she had more children than anyone else and she was the most beautiful woman there.

During the worship service, the boys often stared at her and wished that she were one of those women who nursed their babies in church. But this beautiful woman was so shy it was not likely she would show her breasts in church. Or anywhere else where the boys might see them.

One Communion Sunday the minister invited some of the congregation over to the parsonage for coffee after church. Service always lasted long on Communion Sundays because it took a long time for the minister to pour the wine from the big silver pitcher into all the Communion cups. The grown-ups drank the wine very quickly that morning so the minister knew how tired they were from sitting on those hard church benches. He was being nice by inviting them to come over to the soft chairs in the parsonage, but, of course, it was his beautiful wife who would have to make coffee for all those people.

The boys were standing in the porch watching all the grown-ups finding chairs in the parlor when they saw the minister's wife go into the kitchen with her newest baby. Maybe she was going to nurse it! The boys peeked through the kitchen door. She was nursing all right, but she was so shy that even in her kitchen she had covered her breast and the baby's face with a dish towel.

Later the boys came back for a second try. They smelled freshly-brewed coffee as they sneaked up and didn't expect to see anything unusual. With one hand the minister's wife was lifting one cup after another, and with the other hand she was holding one of her breasts. She squeezed some of her milk into each of the cups.

Pretty soon she served the coffee to her guests. Everyone held the cups on their laps until all the guests were served. Then they raised their cups to their lips together, the same way they did in church with the wine cups, but now no one

17

was saying *This do in remembrance* of anything. Everyone was nodding and saying nice things about the coffee. The minister's wife blushed, as she always did when the congregation showed that they appreciated her.

That night, back home as the boys got ready for bed, one of them said, Say, do you remember what her breast looked like?

None of them did.

I remember something, said the youngest boy. There were 48 cups and nobody had to ask for more.

WHO USED THE WIND
TO ADVANTAGE

When this woman sliced a loaf of bread, she held it under her left breast and with a big knife in her right hand she sliced the bread into big pieces. She sliced straight up toward her breast so that it looked like she was going to slice right into her breast.

That was one thing that made people notice this woman. Another thing was the time a strong wind blew the clothes off the clothesline. When she went outside to get them, they were nowhere to be seen. Her husband said it was thieves and wanted to call the sheriff. But this woman said, Wait a minute.

She took an armful of newspapers and hung them on the clothesline. When the wind blew the newspapers away, she followed them, out across the fields and wherever the wind took them. The wind led her to the clothes. Pretty soon she came back to the house carrying them.

Some neighbor men were there and they stood watching with her husband as she carried the big armload of clothes. But none of the men praised her for being so clever. Just as they didn't say anything about the way she sliced bread.

Any good hunter knows how to use the wind, said one of the men.

Sailors too, said another, while the woman sat quietly in her chair folding the clothes.

MOLEY

On Saturdays the boys liked to go into town and watch the midget shoe repairman named Moley sit on his high stool tapping nails. It was best to watch him before lunch, before he went to the tavern where he drank a lot of beer and ran around the pool table, drunk, with a little stool to stand on when he shot.

When Moley drank too much beer too many weeks in a row, people got angry with him and didn't bring him their shoes anymore. You could tell how much beer he was drinking by seeing how bad people's shoes looked on the street.

Then one day Moley .quit drinking beer. This was after many weeks of the boys' going to watch him tapping nails but not finding him in his shop.

When Moley quit drinking beer, he wanted everyone to know about it. So he started drinking half-gallon cans of tomato and grapefruit juice and stacking the empty cans in his little shop. When people stopped by his shop now, he counted the juice cans for them and they were supposed to know from this how much beer he wasn't drinking.

"Ninety-nine cans last count" was the word, and everyone brought their shoes.

Those were good Saturdays for the boys. They could go to Moley's shop at any time of the day and see his little hands go down inside a shoe to find its problem. Sometimes, to show they liked him, the boys helped stack the cans in tens to make the counting easy.

But one Saturday, in the middle of the winter, after Moley's shop had gotten so full of juice cans that you could hardly get inside, the boys came to his shop door and it was locked. Through the windows they saw that all the juice cans were gone.

Of course, Moley had taken to beer again and had cleaned out the juice cans to make no secret of it. Still he had built up enough good will during those juice days that his shelves were packed with shoes that needed him—credit enough waiting there for months of good times in the tavern.

WHO TALKED TO HIS BEES

The beekeeper was always talking. He sounded as if he had as much to say as his bees in apple blossom season. But all he talked about was what he was doing:

Now I'm moving this hive over just a bit. There. Now I'm checking the angle toward the sun. There. Now I'm walking to the clover field to see what we have this year.

He went on like this all day long, day after day, while the bees went buzzing about their business as if he didn't exist.

One day a blind pastor was walking through the country hoping to hear a voice from heaven. When he walked past the beekeeper's place, he heard a strange voice over the buzzing of the bees.

The blind pastor stopped to listen more carefully. The sound of the bees was like the golden pillars of heaven in his mind, and the voice of the beekeeper was like the Lord Himself descending from heaven.

I am listening, said the blind pastor. Now he heard the voice of the beekeeper again, saying, I am going to wipe the sweat from my forehead. There.

The blind pastor trembled, fearing that he was a cause for the Lord's perspiring. Falling to his knees, he said, Have I been such a labor to Thee, Lord?

My nose itches, said the beekeeper. I'm going to move my wrist slowly up to it and rub it a bit. There.

Now the blind pastor feared that he was an offensive odor to the sensitive nostrils of the Lord.

Does my earthly body offend Thee, Lord?

Just then the beekeeper heard the blind pastor and turned to see who it was. The sight of the blind pastor kneeling along the road with his hands stretched toward the sky was so strange that the beekeeper stopped talking for the first time in many days.

With that, several bees came down on him and stung him, since this beekeeper never wore any netting to protect himself. The beekeeper screamed and swore in pain, then ran as fast as he could to find some mud before the swelling began.

The blind pastor, hearing the ungodly commotion, sprang to his feet, vowing never to wander through the country again.

He started walking slowly back toward town where every Sunday he preached two sermons.

The beekeeper resolved to mend his ways also and never to stop talking in the presence of his bees again, no matter how great the distraction.

The bees went on buzzing in their usual way, since, for them, this was a very busy time of the year.

WHO HAD SIX TOES

One of the girls at school had six toes on one foot.

Did you hear about Maggie's toes? asked one girl who didn't like her.

What? said one of the boys. And that was it for Maggie. Soon everyone at school knew she had six toes on one foot. At first they just watched her as she walked, trying to figure out which foot had all those toes.

Then they teased her. Hey, Maggie, what are you hiding in your shoe? one boy asked.

Six toes, said Maggie. Want to see them?

Yes! shouted everyone, not teasing anymore.

First, I should tell you, said Maggie, it is a magic toe.

The boys started to snicker.

It can give you a tooth ache. Or an ear ache. It can make you cross-eyed. It will give you diarrhea if it wants to.

Nobody snickered anymore because Maggie got all A's in school and probably knew what she was saying.

Will it hurt us if we look at it? said one of the boys.

Maybe not, said Maggie.

Maggie took off her shoe and then her sock. It was the left foot. Most of the boys had guessed wrong. And there sat the extra toe on Maggie's little white foot. It was smaller than the others and sat piggy-back between the second and third toes.

Can you wiggle it? asked one of the boys in a whisper.

If I want to, said Maggie.

Do you want to? he whispered again, with much respect.

Yes, said Maggie, And she wiggled her magic toe.

Just then, the girl who had told everyone about Maggie's extra toe ran away crying and holding her hands over her ears.

WHO WERE POOR AND CRAZY

There was a family of poor and crazy people who lived in a house close to the railroad track. They were a father, a mother, and a little girl. They were all crazy and let their mouths hang open as if they were too tired to keep them closed. You could always see their tongues. They had big tongues.

In the summer you'd see them at all the softball games, at the Fireman's Ball, at the country fairs, at the circus, at the 4th-of-July picnic. They'd hitch-hike to all the celebrations, and people picked them up.

But in the winter they always stayed home. When there was a blizzard, neighbors went over there with food to make sure they stayed alive.

One morning after a snow storm the boys went along to bring food to these poor and crazy people. The car had to follow the snow plow to get there that day. Then the boys pushed the baskets of food over the snow as they climbed along over the big drifts.

There was a screen porch at the front of the house. When the boys got the baskets of food up on it, they slipped on the ice on the porch floor. Water didn't make that ice. It was urine. Urine that ran across the porch floor when the chamber pot got full. The pot sat next to the front door.

What must have happened was they didn't feel like emptying the pot in the cold winter weather and pretty soon it was too late even if they wanted to. The pot was frozen down and everything in it was frozen solid. So they just kept using it, and it got fuller and fuller with the crazy people's urine and dung—which kept freezing every time they used it. Now it was so full that a big mound had grown on top. A mound that went straight up to a point where the last person had used it.

The boys knocked on the door and waited for the crazy people to come and get the food.

Say, said the biggest boy, pointing at the pot with its big mound, That would remind me of an ice cream cone if it wasn't so cold out here.

Stupid, said the smallest boy. If it wasn't so cold out here, it wouldn't be there.

WHO WASHED EGGS EVERY NIGHT

One old man went out every night to a small shed behind the house where he washed eggs. There was no electricity in the shed and he lit a kerosene lantern, which he liked to do because it reminded him of the old days.

In this shed he sat on a little stool and washed eggs with a worn wash cloth and put each egg into a large egg crate. He washed a whole crate of eggs every night!

But people knew he didn't like to wash eggs. What he really wanted was for people to come and visit him. So people did that, every night, and the shed filled up with visitors who came to see the egg washer.

They also wanted to see the man's friendly rat which came out through a hole in the floor. The man threw an egg at the rat when it appeared. This was their game.

The old man would say, Hah! I'll get you this time, you slimy critter! and he'd throw an egg at the rat. The rat always ducked into its hole and Splat! the egg hit the wall. Then the rat came back out and ate the egg.

Everyone laughed and liked to see the old man and his rat play their game. The rat had gotten very fat from eating all those eggs and its coat was smooth and silky. When it finished eating, it pushed the egg shell down the hole with its nose so the old man wouldn't have to clean it up. Then it sat on its hind legs hoping the old man would throw another egg.

The man grumbled about how weak his old arms were, that they weren't even strong enough anymore to hit a rat with an egg.

But one night the visitors heard him say, You know, it's getting so's I know that rat better than my wife.

II

What Started
Walking Home from School

WHAT STARTED
WALKING HOME FROM SCHOOL

One spring day the boys stopped on their way home from school to drink water from a puddle along the road. They used sheets from their spelling workbooks to make paper cups.

Except one.

He knelt down and drank straight from the puddle. This way he could see his face as he drank.

The others looked into their paper cups before they drank. This way they could see if there were any snakes in the water.

The one who drank kneeling down swallowed a snake. He saw its tail in the water between his eyes, but it was too late. The head was already down his throat.

When he stood up, the boys with paper cups said, You swallowed a snake, didn't you!

The boy who swallowed the snake said he had not. He said the water tasted good the way he drank it from the puddle.

The other boys teased him and said his eyes looked different. The boy who swallowed the snake knelt down again and looked into the puddle. He saw a snake. Maybe it was another snake. Maybe it was the snake he had swallowed. Maybe he looked that way now. He told the other boys he did not look different.

As they walked home, the boy felt the snake curl up in his stomach and go to sleep. This will be easy, he thought.

For supper, he said he was not hungry. He drank one glass of warm milk. The snake woke up and drank the warm milk, then fell asleep again.

When the boy went to bed, he saw that his stomach was bigger. So he slept on his back with his hands over his stomach to keep the snake warm. That night his dreams were different from anyone's.

The next day no one asked him about the snake.

THE HORNETS' NEST

The leaves had fallen and with them a hornets' nest. The boys found pieces of the nest among the oak leaves. It was prettier than the leaves—like beautiful paper, but softer.

It looked like the hornets had put a little bit of everything into that nest. Somebody's blue sock chewed up and weaved in with the yellow flower and red string. All those colors mixed through the color of dead oak leaves. The boys took the pieces out in the sun and touched them and looked at them for a long time.

Then they tried to put them back together and did pretty well. They made wallpaper glue and ground up some leaves to mix with the glue, and fit all the pieces together until it looked just like a hornets' nest. They tied what they had made back up in the tree with some string.

That was also the year the boys repaired their tree house. They found some old shingles and a few two-by-fours nobody was using. They were a little careless putting their own house together, but it held. It was a good year for fixing houses.

In the spring the hornets didn't go back to their nest, but they hung around the boys' tree house more than usual.

AN ALLIGATOR IN THE SANDPIT

No one believed it when it came out in the newspaper that an alligator had been seen in the sandpit.

But sure as can be everybody started watching for it, sitting in the cornfields around the sandpit and watching for that alligator to show itself. Nobody brought guns. That would come later. When somebody really saw that alligator—some place besides the newspaper.

The boys were not allowed out there at night—but on Saturdays, in the daylight, it was okay. And they liked it. It was like fishing—only with your eyes. Sitting there and waiting for a nibble. Waiting for the alligator to make a ripple on the surface like a bobber and tell you it was there.

Do you think anybody saw that alligator? No. Nobody saw it. Not even the boys with their good eyes. Did the newspaper just make that up to be funny? Who knows.

The farmer out there complained that his corn was getting flattened where everybody sat and watched for the alligator. Maybe the alligator died from fright seeing all those people on the shore. Maybe the turtles ate it then.

But everybody got to talking to each other while they watched. It was like they were sitting around a big bonfire. Nobody looked at each other, just at the water as far down as they could see. Pretty soon somebody started singing and then everybody was singing—even on Saturday afternoon when the boys were there. They blushed a little and held hands with people.

This lasted until corn picking time when there was too much to do.

TWO NEGROES
ON THE RAILROAD TRACK

The boys had to pull cockleburs out of the corn that day. Walking down the long rows watching for the little round leaves between the rows or at the base of the corn stalks. When they came to the end of the row, they waited, sometimes sat and rubbed their feet, before starting back. The row ended at the railroad track. That's where they saw the Negroes. Two of them, walking between the rails.

Look! said one of the boys. Negroes on the railroad track!

They stood together, staring, as the Negroes came closer. They had big sacks on their shoulders.

What's in those sacks? whispered one of the boys.

Before they could decide, the Negroes saw them. They smiled and waved at the boys and said, Hello there.

The boys waved.

The Negroes kept going, down the track, looking back now and then as if to check if a train or something else was coming.

The boys couldn't decide whether it was all right for Negroes to be there or whether they should run home and tell somebody. They couldn't decide either what was in the big sacks. It didn't look like anything alive.

Maybe it's cotton they're going to sell somewhere, said one of the boys.

When the Negroes disappeared, the boys walked out on the tracks and looked for footprints. They found a few and took turns putting their own feet in them to see whose feet were closest to being as big.

Then they went back to picking cockleburs, and probably missed a few, because all they could think about was their own footprints following them everywhere.

SUNDAY SCHOOL

The boys went to a very strict church. In Sunday School after the morning service, they had to sit in assigned seats. During the hymn sing the Superintendent checked the seating chart, and anyone who was not present had to memorize Psalm 23, Isaiah 53, or I Corinthians 13.

Not many children liked the Sunday School Superintendent. When he asked the children to suggest a song during the hymn sing, one of the boys always yelled out Page 564. On page 564 was a hymn called Lord, Dismiss Us With Thy Blessing. This made the Superintendent angry, but he never caught the boy who yelled Page 564.

Later the church got modern, but the rules stayed strict. Now all the seats for Sunday School had big numbers painted on them and a camera on the ceiling took pictures automatically. Empty seats showed up as numbers in the picture, and anyone whose number showed had to memorize Psalm 23, Isaiah 53, or I Corinthians 13.

The boys decided to fool the camera. They took balloons to Sunday School, blew them up, and tied them to their seats. This way the numbers didn't show up in the picture. Pretty soon more and more children started tying balloons to their seats instead of going to Sunday School.

After many weeks an Elder of the church decided to visit Sunday School to tell the children how wonderful they were for their good attendance.

When he walked in the back, he saw a sanctuary full of balloons swaying back and forth in the seats, and behind the podium where the Superintendent was supposed to be was the biggest balloon of all swaying slowly on a thick piece of twine.

THE BOYS LEARN ABOUT WATER

People in America don't know anything about water, said the boys' grandfather who had moved from Holland when he was a young man. The boys liked it when he visited because he always had a story to tell, usually about something that was wrong with America.

They knew his rules. They were supposed to listen until he finished telling his story. Then he would ask them a question so they would have a chance to show what they learned.

Let me tell you about water, he said, and the boys sat back to listen.

If you dig a hole and there's water nearby, you should stand between the hole and the water. Because if the water sees the hole it's going to want to go there too. Water has eyes, you know. Very good eyes. That's how it finds its way around so well under the ground.

Now your ocean water, it has eyes too. In Holland, men built dykes to hide the beautiful land. You know that story Americans tell about the Dutch boy who put his finger in the dyke. Well, that little trickle of water wasn't going to hurt anybody. But that Dutch boy knew he had to keep his finger in the eye of the dyke. You mustn't tempt water, you see. If the ocean water got a glimpse of that green grass of Holland, it would all want to be there too. In America you don't know these things. You think everything is blind except for the people who are trying to make it do what they want.

Now, boys, you've been on this farm your whole life—you answer this question. If you want water to stay in the creek, what should you do?

I know. Make sure the bank is so high the water can't see over it, said the oldest boy proudly.

No! shouted the youngest boy.

What is your answer, little one? said the old man.

Pee in it, said the boy. Nothing can see if you pee in its eyes.

And if you had been that little Dutch boy in Holland, what would you have stuck in the dyke? asked the old Dutchman with a twinkle in his eye.

SPRING GRASS

In the spring when the cows were turned out to pasture and ate the new grass, the milk tasted different. That isn't all. The spring grass made their bowels loose.

This was no problem so long as the cows were in the pasture. But when they were in the stancheons, it could be dangerous for someone walking behind them.

One of the boys walked behind a cow one time with a bucket of milk just when the cow coughed. It was like someone slapping him across the face when that cow's loose bowels hit him. And it got all over his clothes and in the bucket of milk he was carrying.

The other boys heard the splattering, and when they saw him, they laughed. So, to show that he was not a sissy, he wiped himself off and then poured that bucket of milk through the strainer right in with the other milk.

This surprised the other boys, and the oldest one said, Won't that give us a bad rating with the creamery?

I don't care, said the boy who had been slapped in the face.

So they waited until the end of the month for the creamery report. It said AVERAGE!

That made all the boys laugh.

What do you think happened to that green milk?

One guessed that an old man was putting it in his tea. Another guessed that it had been made into green cheese. But the guess that they liked the most was that it was made into ice cream and shipped to the city.

The boys sat in a circle laughing for hours about all those city kids who were eating that spring grass ice cream and laughing about farm kids who smelled like manure.

STRANGE SMELLS IN THE NIGHT

One night the boys were getting ready for bed.

I smell a girl, said the smallest boy.

There aren't any girls here, silly, said the biggest boy.

They started looking anyway. Under the beds and inside drawers. One of the window curtains moved a little and the smallest boy said, See, there! That was a girl!

But there were no arms or feet, only the curtain moving a little. The boys went to bed without finding the girl. Still, they could not sleep because they could smell the girl. The smell got stronger.

After a while, in the dark, one of them said, It's not a girl, it's a lady. It smells like a grown lady.

They turned on the lights and looked for the lady. But she was not there.

Back in bed, they lay listening and smelling the strange smell. It's not a girl or a lady, one of them said. It smells like an old, old woman.

Again, the boys turned on the lights. The curtain was still moving. This time they saw something. It was dust, blowing in through the window. So they closed the window and went back to bed.

After that, they fell asleep.

III

Bloating
and Its Remedies

BLOATING AND ITS REMEDIES

One night the cows broke through the fence and got into the alfalfa field. In the morning they were lying in the field bloated. Their stomachs were big mounds, and the hair on their sides looked like grass on a steep hill.

The neighbors came with their remedies. One with a sharpened metal tube which he stuck into the paunch to let the air out. Another with a small hose which he covered with grease and inserted into the anus. Another with a solution of soda and soap which he made the sick cows swallow.

The boys watched the men working on the bloated cows. Soon they wanted to help. But the men would only let them work on one they already had given up for dead. One boy pulled the tail. Another pulled the tongue. The others ran and leaped onto the swollen body. Jumped on it. Kicked. Fought for a place on the top.

The men pointed and laughed at the boys' foolish efforts. But then the cow exploded, belching and farting and coming back to life in gusts of hot alfalfa fumes. Leaping to its feet, bucking and throwing one of the boys into the air. Then it stood there looking mixed up, shaking, and letting the boys stroke its back and rub its ears.

The boys and cow stood there a while, looking at each other, and the boys almost cried at the sight of this resurrection.

Then the men reminded them to go to the house and wash themselves so that they would not smell of it in school.

TEASING THE STEERS

The boys liked to hold out hay toward the steers across the electric fence wire and pull it back when the steers tried to eat it. They kept pulling it back until the steers leaned too far and got a terrible shock. They jumped back without getting any hay. The boys laughed at them and shouted Hi-yah! You stupid animals!

After a while the steers knew they would get a shock if they tried to reach the hay the boys were holding. But the steers came anyway, trying harder every time to get the hay without getting a shock. They always got a shock because the boys pulled the hay away. The steers jumped and sometimes trembled before trying it again.

Pretty soon, the boys got tired of this game. The smallest boy said, Let's see who can urinate closest to the electric fence without getting a shock.

Since he said this, he tried it first. He urinated in an arc over the electric fence and slowly lowered the stream until it was only 3 inches from the electric wire. Then he pinched off the stream in his penis and did not get a shock.

Soon the other boys tried this. One came an inch from the wire and did not get a shock. Each time one of them tried it, he pinched off the stream before it touched the wire. The boys did this daily for many weeks and learned to get very close to the wire with their urine. Sometimes they told stories, between taking turns, about a boy somewhere who urinated on an electric fence wire.

After a while, the steers didn't even come near the boys. Because they weren't holding hay anymore.

THE ROOSTER AND HEN SECRET

Often the boys went out into the yard to watch a rooster and hen mate. They had watched horses mate, and what happened there was no secret to them. The boar mounting the sow left little to be imagined. Dogs, cats, rabbits, sheep, and cattle had very open mating manners. There were no secrets with these animals. The boys could see what was happening.

But try as they did, crawling up behind roosters and hens, peering through knotholes and from behind wagons—from only a few feet away!—they could not figure how they mated. There were those ruffling feathers, the rooster's beak clamped to the comb of the hen, and the cloud of dust they made doing it. But what they were doing remained a cloud of mystery.

When the butchering season came, the boys wanted to help clean chickens. Surely, this would be a way to discover the secrets of rooster and hen. They looked closely at each tail feather as they plucked it, thinking that somewhere they would find the quill that was more than a quill. They looked closely at the plucked carcass. They could not find the answer.

Later, the boys became men and found wives. Some nights, alone with their wives in dark farmhouses on the plains, they confessed their ignorance of chickens. The wives forgave them their ignorance and often confessed that they too did not know.

Sometimes these husbands and wives, even today, in the privacy of each others' eyes, suggest that maybe no one knows how chickens mate.

Do you?

FEWER CATS NOW

Fifty cats were not too many on the farm. Sixty or seventy, it was all right. They were worth their weight in cream. Plenty of cats meant more corn in the corn crib. Because cats ate the rats. Rats ate too many times their weight in corn. Cats were worth whatever they ate. Besides the rats.

This was before rat poison. Rat poison cost less than cream for the cats. And worked faster. Cats were like people that way, and rat poison was like machines. So rat poison was in and cats were out. The only thing was—boys couldn't play with rat poison.

So they couldn't make parachutes for the cats anymore and drop them from the top of the windmill. They used to do that —a harness and twine and feed sacks. This worked pretty well for most of the cats. The ones that liked it. The ones that purred when they were carried up the ladder to the top. These were the ones that didn't fight back when the boys dropped them from the top. They had a good ride down and were happy to do it again.

Some of the cats fought when they were falling and tried to climb up the parachute. That killed them. But there were so many cats in those days that nobody missed one if it got killed this way. That was before rat poison.

Now the cats get spayed because there is no reason to have so many. There are so few that if one got killed in a parachute, everyone would ask, Where is that cat? Lots of rat poison and lots of corn, and the price of cream going up. Only two or three cats left, and they sit on the front porch. Eating cat food and getting sick a lot.

DUCKS AND BACON RIND

Well, everyone always told the boys not to feed bacon rind to the ducks, but nobody told the boys why not.

So they took some raw bacon rind and threw it to the ducks. A big duck swallowed it. The boys followed that duck around, watching to see what would happen. The duck looked all right.

But then the duck stopped, ruffled its wings, and shat the bacon rind onto the ground. Up waddled another duck and swallowed the bacon rind. Soon this duck shat it out, and another swallowed it.

This went on for a while, and the ducks learned to follow the last duck that had swallowed the rind, waiting for it to come out so they'd have their turn at it.

The boys watched the bacon rind being passed around from one duck to another in this way until one of them got an idea.

Let's tie a string to the bacon, he said.

The other boys looked surprised when they saw in their minds what would happen.

The boys chuckled and ran to get some strong string. After they tied this to the rind, they went back to the ducks. The first duck swallowed it, then the second, and so on, until the boys had all the ducks on the string. They held it tight, pulling the bacon rind tight against the arse of the last duck.

Later the boys told this story to the men.

That would make a good story to tell some city slickers, said one of the men, knowing it never happened.

THE BOYS LEARN TO USE WIRE

Sometimes a sow couldn't have her young. They'd catch in the tight opening of her womb.

When the men saw this happening, they called the boys. The boys' little hands and thin arms were just right for reaching deep into the sow to where the pigs were stuck.

First one of them soaped-up, rubbing soap on one hand and arm up to his shoulder. Then he'd go in shoulder-deep to find the little snout. When he felt the snout, he'd pinch it between his fingers.

The problem was that both his hand and the pig snout were slippery and he couldn't hang on if the pig was stuck very tight at all.

Then one boy got the idea to use a heavy wire as long as his arm with a little hook on the end that slipped over his forefinger. He went in with this and hooked the pig under the chin.

The other boys helped, pulling the wire from the outside.

Sometimes the wishbone jaw shattered and the pig died, but when it worked the pig came fast. The boys hurried to pick it up and put it bleeding to the sow's teats.

That little bit of pain made the pig lively from the start and the blood quickly got washed away by that fresh white milk.

THE OLD BOAR AND THE PIGS

One time a sow that had nine little pigs ate a piece of glass and died. Her pigs quickly started to wither. The boys did what they could to save those pigs—feeding them cow's milk from a bottle and giving them little bits of sod—but nothing worked. The pigs got the scours, their hair got scruffy, and their hind legs got so weak that their rear quarters weaved when they tried to walk.

Then one night an old boar broke into the pen with the little pigs. In the morning he was lying with the sick little animals and grunting like a sow.

Get out of there, you stupid boar! the boys shouted.

But the old boar just growled and snapped at them.

Go on, you can't give them any milk!

Of course, the boar did not understand them. But when he saw that the boys did not dare to come into the pen with him, he lay down and turned his large belly toward the pigs the way a sow does.

The pigs nestled up against that old boar and started to suck on his useless little teats.

What a funny sight! thought the boys, though they were sure the pigs couldn't be getting any milk. But soon the pigs looked stronger than they had the night before. They fought over nipples and squealed like healthy little pigs. The boys didn't know what to think of this, but since the pigs were so happy with the old boar they let them alone.

The next morning the boys ran to the hoghouse to see how the old boar was doing with the pigs. The pigs were lying against his big belly and he was snoring loudly. When he heard the boys, he stood up growling and all the pigs rolled off his belly into the straw, dead.

The old boar sniffed the dead pigs for a moment and then ate one. Soon he went back into the pig yard and lay down in a big wallow, grunting like an old boar again, but not mean anymore.

THE FIRST-CALF HEIFER

There was a young heifer that was trying to have her first calf. She lay in the barn tossing her head, heaving, and stiffening her legs, but nothing came out.

The boys stood behind her watching for the front hooves to appear, the tongue between them, and then the nostrils. They had helped lots of calves come into the world before, taking hold of the front feet and pulling when the cow heaved, one time helping with the block-and-tackle when one was too long in coming.

But this one was different. There were no feet showing to take hold of or tie on to. When the heifer pushed hard, they could see part of the calf—a black and white holstein—but no front feet. They couldn't tell for sure what part of the calf was showing through the heifer's small opening.

After a few hours the men were there trying to figure out what to do. One man with small hands worked his arm in when the heifer was not pushing. He couldn't figure it out. Things were twisted around and none of the parts were the way they should be for a calf to be born. One hoof was pointed up against the spine, and the man with small hands couldn't move it.

Pretty soon it looked as if the heifer was going to die. She quit trying and lay there waiting for the men to do something.

This calf doesn't want to be born! shouted the man with small hands, and he pulled as hard as he could at the wedged parts. Then he went in with his jackknife and started cutting parts of the calf off and pulling them out.

We're going to have two dead ones if I don't get this out of there, he said. He hurried with his jackknife, cutting off parts that were stuck, pulling them out and putting them into a feed sack which the other men had brought. When all the stuck parts were cut off, what was left slipped out like an egg yolk. The men put this into the sack too. As soon as the heifer looked all right, the men went to the house for coffee.

The boys stayed with the heifer a while, waiting for the afterbirth to come. But instead, the heifer heaved once and the head of another calf appeared. The boys grabbed its front legs and pulled. This calf came out so fast that the two boys fell over backwards and the calf landed on their laps. The boys laughed to see a calf that was not all cut up into pieces. They rubbed the new calf with straw and let it suck their fingers. It was a healthy bull calf, and they led it to the heifer's teats. It was very hungry from waiting all this time to get out.

When the new calf had drunk its fill, the boys decided to play a joke on the men. They carried the calf outside and called, Come look! Come look! One of the boys had emptied the sack behind the barn so he was holding a bloody empty sack for the men to see.

When the men ran out to see what was happening, the oldest boy said, We decided to put that calf back together! Then they put the new calf down and it walked.

But the men were not fooled for a minute. By God, she had twins, the man with the small hands said.

Still, it was a good joke, and the boys teased the men with it for a long time after that.

THE BIG PUSH

One morning the boys walked into the cow barn to find an awful sight. One of the cows had calved the night before, but during the night her womb had come out and was lying in the gutter behind the cow.

The biggest boy didn't gag or jump back, and he was the first to notice that the strange mass led into the cow. He stayed and watched while the other boys ran for help.

Then the work began. The womb had to be cleaned off with soap and kept clean so that the insides of the cow would not get infected. The the hardest part was shoving the womb back in. Pushing the womb back in is like trying to push a calf back in—nothing inside the cow wants things to go in reverse like that.

When the boys understood what they were working with, the womb in the gutter did not bother their stomachs. First, they cleaned the gutter around the womb with pitch forks and then with water. They got down on their knees and started washing the womb, pulling the clean part up on their laps as they worked. When this was finished, they cradled the womb in a white sheet and got ready to help with the big push.

All of this took several hours and word got around the neighborhood. Even the mailman stopped in to see this and was ready to help push. The boys had to stand back, but the men's hands were so big that they couldn't get enough of them around the cow's vagina to tuck the womb in as they pushed.

So the boys got their turn. And they thought of something the men wished they had. One of them went around to the front and fed the cow some oats while the others pushed. Having things coming in from both ends at the same time must have confused the cow's instincts. When she was swallowing the oats, the boys behind pushed. The cow coughed the oats up but the womb was in. After that the cow ate the oats again without coughing it up. The womb stayed in too.

That's the end of the story. But boys have dreams and cows have dreams. Think about that for a while.

AN UNEXPECTED BLIZZARD

One winter night a blizzard came when no one was expecting it. Some pregnant sows that were not penned up got caught in that blizzard. A few knew it was time to come in and were safe in the hog house the next morning.

But most of the sows stayed out in the blizzard and disappeared under the snow drifts.

The boys went out as soon as they heard there would be no school and started helping find the buried sows. They were lighter than the men, so they walked over the snowbanks without sinking down. They used sticks to poke through the snow, and could tell when they hit a sow—it moved! Sometimes making the stick jump right back out of the snow!

Here's one! one of the boys would call. The men would come with big feed scoops to dig the sow out and get it safe into the hog house.

Pretty soon the boys had found all the buried sows. Except one. There was one sow missing.

They went back with their sticks, poking everywhere in the pig lot where the sows might be lying. The men helped. Everyone poking in the snowbanks for the lost sow. After several hours, they guessed that it must be dead and that even if they were poking it, it wasn't moving.

The boys sat up late that night, feeling bad that they had not found the lost sow. The next morning there was more snow, so all the tracks and stick marks were covered up. The boys had to give up, but they still thought about that sow.

Three weeks later there was a big thaw. The boys watched for the body of the lost sow to start showing through the snow. They couldn't figure out what spot they could have missed with their sticks, poking.

At noon one Saturday, the lost sow stood up, broke through the dirty melting snow and stood there wobbling. And she had little pigs! Six of them still alive, and though the sow was skinny the little pigs were fine—tugging at her dugs as she tried to walk away.

The men put the sow in a special pen with a heat lamp on her. The boys carried the little pigs to the house and put them in a box by the stove to get them warm and fed them milk from a bottle before bringing them back to the sow.

What happens to animals that are so lucky like this? one of the boys asked.

I don't know, said another.

The boys watched the pigs grow up. These pigs were very special to the boys, but pretty soon they hardly looked any different from the other pigs.

When they were big enough, they were sent to market with the other pigs. And somebody somewhere was eating that special meat, and not even knowing it.

THE OLD TURTLE

One day a farmer found a dead cow in his pasture. Its throat had been torn and slashed by something. The sheriff looked at it. The paper said something about it. Pretty soon everybody had a story about it.

The boys listened to the men talking—and one thing they heard was that a long time ago when that farmer was a boy on that same farm, he found a big turtle near the creek that ran through the pasture where the cow was killed. He told his father about it—and the two of them went out there with shovels and beat that big turtle's head on a rock. They left it there, to return after sunset when they were sure it was dead. They were going to make turtle soup when it was safe to pick up that big turtle.

When they came there after sunset, the turtle was gone. They found its claw marks in the mud along the creek where it had pulled itself back to the water. They didn't see it again.

Did that turtle come back 25 years later to get even? Kill a cow in that same pasture where its head had been beaten flat?

Sure enough. Somebody found that old turtle. Or at least saw it. Its head was like a dish pan, flat like that, and its jaws were a lot broader than they should have been. Everybody put one and one together.

You could read about this later in Ripley's "Believe it or Not." That's the whole story.

The boys didn't talk about it much. It didn't have much to do with them since there weren't that many turtles left in the creeks anymore. Even Old Dish Pan Head would probably be dead pretty soon. Before it got any more cows. Cut worm or gopher poison would get in its water—or some new weed spray that hadn't been tested on turtles.

THE BLIND PONY

The pony was blind in one eye when it was born. At first it was easy to catch if you remembered which side to come up on. But after a while the ear on the blind side got strong from listening so hard for someone sneaking up on it. That ear got so good it would hear someone coming on the blind side farther than the good eye could see on the other.

So the boys had to think of new ways to catch the blind pony. First they tried trapping it in the corner of the pasture, but the blind pony always ran with its good eye towards the fence and its good ear towards the boys. This way it never ran into the fence and could still whip its head when it heard the lasso coming through the air. Also, the blind pony was a good kicker, and the boys learned not to try grabbing at it from behind.

Next the boys tried hiding in trees where the pony walked, thinking that they could drop a rope over its head as it passed under them. But it was as if the pony could hear that part of the tree where the leaves weren't rustling and wouldn't walk under a tree where one of the boys was hiding.

Finally, the boys tried coaxing the blind pony with apples.

Why didn't we think of this before! said one of the boys when this worked. Pretty soon the blind pony came at the sound of the boys climbing the apple trees. Its nose got strong too, and it could tell which boy had an apple in his pocket.

But the boys never did saddle or bridle it. They knew how dangerous it was to ride a blind pony.

THE ALBINO FOX

Everybody had seen the albino fox a time or two. Especially in winter when, instead of hiding against the snow, it lay on clear spots on the dark plowed fields and basked in the sun.

What would a patch of white snow be doing on the side of a plowed hill where all the rest of the snow had melted?

Someone would get out his binoculars, and, sure enough, it would be the albino fox.

You couldn't find anyone who didn't want to shoot that albino fox and stuff it for a trophy. But nobody could get close enough for a good shot. It always got up in time and ran for the snow where it disappeared like a drift in the wind.

I want to get those pink eyes in my sights, said one farmer who had been hunting the albino fox for years. So he bought three greyhound dogs that cost him a lot of money. He also bought a big scope for his rifle.

The neighbors came to look at his dogs and rifle scope and wondered if he could really do it. Everyone said they would telephone him if they saw the fox.

Nobody's going to get that tricky white fox. That white fox is too clever, they said.

The next time someone saw the albino fox, they telephoned the man with the dogs. And the neighbors followed him in their cars as he drove off in his pickup with the greyhounds and new scope.

He let the dogs out on one side of the hill and went to wait on the other side—a half mile from where the albino fox was basking in the sun on the plowed field.

The dogs got the scent of the fox right away and caught up with it in no time at all. The fox looked like a cripple when those fast dogs were after it. The dogs played with the albino fox, throwing it in the air and letting it run a little ways before catching it again. That fox was so mixed up that it ran toward the man with the big scope. Pretty soon the fox and dogs were so close that the man called off his dogs. The fox sat in the snow panting and the man found its pink eyes in his new scope.

That sure was easy, said one farmer who was watching.

Ever try shooting the broad side of a barn from the inside? teased another farmer.

I'll bet you'd have good luck hunting sheep with those dogs, said another.

The man who shot the albino fox felt so foolish that he hid his trophy in the cellar. But it was too late. He could just as well have kept it in his living room because nobody came to visit him anymore anyhow.

THE INJURED FAWN

The boys were walking along a headline fence one summer day. In the grass they found a fawn that had crawled out of the alfalfa field where a mower had cut off one of its hind legs and almost cut off the other.

The fawn lay its ears back, hiding, until it knew the boys saw it, then looked up and bleated like a hungry lamb. One of the boys looked for the cut-off leg in the alfalfa but couldn't find it.

They carried the fawn home and fed it milk from a calf bucket that had a rubber nipple on the bottom. After it was fed, the fawn tried to run away, as if it thought a little bit of milk would make its hind legs come back. And somehow it did manage one leap forward, but then fell on its side and didn't try to get up.

Pretty soon, the boys had to tell the men about the fawn they had found. They told the men they wanted to make a new leg for the fawn and sew back the one that was almost cut off. The men said they would help.

The wounds were cleaned with water and black horse salve. The one leg was sewn back and a wooden splint put on it. The other, which was only a stump, got a leather patch put over the exposed bone and a wooden leg the shape of a deer's strapped on.

The boys fed and played with the fawn all summer where it lived in the barn. Towards fall it was so good on its new legs that it jumped and ran, first playing with the boys and then always going for a door or window. The boys had to move quickly to keep it from getting away on its new legs.

With all its jumping and running, the fawn's legs got infected. Gangrene set in and it died.

Did anybody cry? Nobody cried. The boys buried the fawn in the orchard and kept the wooden leg to show people later how it had gotten worn smooth from that fawn's being so happy.

THE PET SQUIRREL

The boys started sneaking kernels of corn out on the back porch for the squirrels. One of the squirrels got very tame. It ran up within a few feet of the boys when they threw corn out to it. After a while, it ate right from their hands.

That's when they told the grown-ups about the squirrel, now that it would be too late for them to say it was foolish wasting corn on a squirrel that would never want to be a pet anyhow.

The grown-ups liked the pet squirrel too.

Then it started sitting on the kitchen window sill. And came right in the house when the window was open.

The pet squirrel moved in.

Almost any time you might see it sitting on the back of a chair, listening to the radio, or in the kitchen drinking from the sink.

Towards fall, one of the boys yelled, Who put nuts in my coat pockets?

The other boys checked their coat pockets too. The pockets were full of nuts.

One day the radio sounded strange. The boys found nuts packed in the back between the tubes. The squirrel was reminding everyone to get ready for winter.

So the boys checked their mittens to make sure they didn't have any holes in them. And their overshoes to make sure they didn't leak. The squirrel kept busy stuffing nuts into everything.

What a smart squirrel, said one of the boys.

Then, one October day, something strange happened. The boys found the pet squirrel dead on the kitchen floor. What had happened was it had gotten up in the cupboard and tried to get into a box of Post Toasties. It didn't know the box would topple when it got all its weight on the top. The fall didn't kill the squirrel, but the corner of the box landed right on its head when they hit the floor together. The boys found a little dent above its eye. The squirrel was covered with Post Toasties.

So, in the cold fall air, the boys carried the squirrel to the garden to bury it.

Look, said one of the boys, pointing into the trees. The other squirrels were watching.

There sat the other squirrels, shivering on the bare branches.

Maybe this squirrel wasn't so smart after all, said one of the boys, shovelling dirt over it.

DEATH DEATH DEATH

One hot summer day the boys were wandering around the yard.

What's that smell? asked one of them.

Hog manure is what it is, said another.

No, look, said the first boy. It's that dead chicken.

Sure enough, there was a dead chicken lying near the chicken coop. It had been dead maybe a week and the sun had eaten most of its insides out.

Then another boys said, No, look. Maybe the smell is coming from that dead pig over there.

The boys walked over to the dead pig that was lying near the hog house. There were flies all over its body and going in and out of its nose and ears. It was only two days dead so the smell was not very strong yet.

Then another one of the boys said, I'll bet the smell is from that dead starling the cats killed and wouldn't eat. They walked over to the auto shed and found the dead starling, but it was almost dried out to a skeleton.

Death, Death, Death, said one of the boys.

There were dead animals all over the farmyard—if they'd look for them. Besides the rodents that were dead under the ground and they'd never see. Dead flies here and there. Dead grasshoppers in the tall grass. Dead bees. Dead ladybugs. Probably birds that were dying in their nests.

And this was not unusual. Things die. It's just that the boys happened to be noticing it all at once. Which happens in the summer. What was good about winter was that the snow hid dead animals and other dead creatures.

Look. One of the boys pointed to the sky. They were not alone, noticing all the death. A chicken hawk was circling overhead. Circling over the whole farmyard.

This place stinks like dead everything, said one of the boys.

There's only one thing to do about all this death, said the smallest boy. Clothespins. So they put clothespins on their noses and ran off to play.

JIM HEYNEN was born July 14, 1940, on a farm near Sioux Center, Iowa, the second son of first-generation Dutch-American parents. After spending the first eighteen years of his life on the farm, he attended and graduated from Calvin College in Grand Rapids, Michigan. He has done graduate work at the Universities of Oregon and Iowa and lived for some time in South Dakota studying the Sioux Indian language and culture. In 1974 he received the National Endowment for the Arts Fellowship Award in poetry and in 1977 was selected as a U.S.-U.K. Bicentennial Exchange Fellow to Norwich, England. He has taught at the Universities of Iowa, Oregon, Michigan, and Alaska and given workshops and readings in the Midwest and Northwest. Currently, he is directing writing programs for the Centrum Foundation at Fort Worden State Park in Washington.